KEEPING CHRISTMAS

by
BO BAKER

Illustrated by

Marilyn Goss

Keeping Christmas (Expanded Edition)
©1996 by BO Baker
All Rights Reserved
Stonebridge Publisher
P. O. Box 311
McKinney, Texas 75070-0311

Library of Congress Cataloging-in-Publication Data

BO Baker, 1923-
Keeping Christmas (Expanded Edition)/ BO Baker

Subject Heading: Christmas Essays, Poetry,
Devotional material for Christmas addresses.

Library of Congress Catalogue Card Number:

Unless otherwise noted, Scripture quotations are from the
King James Version of the Bible. Scripture quotations
marked (RSV) are from The Revised Standard Version.

Other books by BO Baker:
Made For the Mountains (Word)
Keeping Christmas (Original Edition)
The Lift Of Love (Broadman)
Hangeth In There

Printed By Taylor Publishing Company
1550 Mockingbird
Dallas, Texas 75235

DEDICATION

To all the grandchildren who have brought "ten thousand joys" to our celebration of Christmas, and who will extend those joys and family traditions to kinsmen yet unborn.

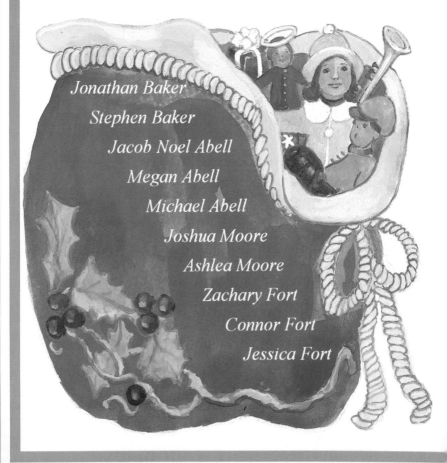

Jonathan Baker

Stephen Baker

Jacob Noel Abell

Megan Abell

Michael Abell

Joshua Moore

Ashlea Moore

Zachary Fort

Connor Fort

Jessica Fort

ACKNOWLEDGMENTS

Paul, the Apostle, reflecting upon the many individuals who contributed to his life and mission exclaimed, "I am debtor...".

I can most certainly identify with his meaningful expression. It would be difficult to number all of those who have so graciously and unselfishly shared in the production of *Keeping Christmas*; nevertheless, I would feel less than replete should I fail to acknowledge my appreciation to special individuals who have made this book a reality.

Perhaps I should begin with the reminder that this is an **expanded edition** of my earlier book by the same title. The book was generously received and copies of the original *Keeping Christmas* have long since become unavailable. With the continuation of years has come not only hurts and harms, but also bright new joys to accent and color my life's swift changing landscapes. I count myself fortunate indeed to have had the love and laughter of my wife Ruth, God's gift to me for what Browning calls "the best of life". She has been a constant source of gentle persuasion, always encouraging me to put my love affair with Christmas in print.

Those who know me well know that I have a great capacity for genuine caring and friendship. I do not forget, nor take lightly the kindnesses, the warmth that well-timed cheering has brought down the little lanes of my journeying. Therefore I begin by expressing my indebtedness to Marilyn Goss who "made time" to fashion the beautifully inviting dust cover of *Keeping Christmas*. She has included a number of her original art pieces in the book and has illustrated selected portions with her very special hallmark of creativity. As a Britisher would say, "She has done a lovely thing."

Dr. Presnall Wood, former editor of *The Baptist Standard*, is deserving of my heartfelt "thank you." It was he who provided the long standing invitation for my Christmas letters to be published and featured in the *Baptist Standard's* Christmas edition.

I extend appreciation to Jan Dickson, "the teacher's teacher," for reading the manuscript and for her helpful suggestions. How deeply I am indebted to my former secretary and "honorary editor", Maxine Off, who has typed, arranged, and edited the manuscript. Her spirit of confidence in me and in the value of the book will always be remembered with humble gratitude. Thank you, my good, good friend.

Also, I express a sincere word of appreciation to Maxine's husband, Mr. Joseph Off, a superb business executive whose "know how" within the marketplace has been extremely helpful in expanding my concept of publication possibilities. Lastly, but certainly not the least in importance, is my acknowledgment and expression of abiding love to my daughter, Dr. Lisa Carol Baker, for her very personal and insightful writing of the Foreword for *Keeping Christmas*. This has pleased me more than words can convey. I'm sure other daughters have written in similar manner but I have no knowledge of it. What else can I say...I'm overwhelmed.

And now, for all who have trimmed my tree with garlands of inspiration-everlasting, left its branches filled with fellowship rich and warm, placed around it gifts of unconditional love, reminders of the Christmas Christ, I do most humbly confess, "I am debtor..."

BO Baker

Stonebridge, 1996

CONTENTS

FOREWORD

Christmas has always been my favorite time of year -- but then I was BO Baker's daughter, so it could hardly be anything else. I have never known anyone who loved Christmas as much as my dad (except perhaps my mother). I remember more than one Christmas morning as a child when he awakened *me* because he could wait no longer to open presents. In matters of the church, my dad has always been the model of decorum and confidentiality. Regarding Christmas gifts, however, he is a terrible Secret-keeper. To this day I have to beg him not to let me in on all my Christmas surprises before Labor Day has come and gone.

My parents passed on a legacy at Christmastime of unbridled festivity and extravagant love. Candles were lit daily; homemade goodies were piled high on cabinets too full to hold them all; Fred Waring's Christmas album played constantly, and of course, a fire blazed in the fireplace even if the air conditioner had to be turned on discretely to defy the Texas heat. My father knows the value of rituals and understands a child's need to have things the same way year after year after year. We were as religious about the special Christmas fruit salad with Royal Anne pitted cherries as we were about the gospel account of Jesus' birth.

It was all part of BO Baker setting the stage, you see. And there was never any doubt who was the main character. We understood even as young children that the joy of jingle bells and Rudolph was only possible because "God so loved the world that He gave His only begotten Son." It is well known that children take their cues from their parents. My brothers and I knew that the gift Dad and Mother would like the best was a nativity scene, which we offered them piece by piece for most of my growing-up years. The figures stayed on a shelf in the living room all year round, the only decorations that did not get boxed away in the attic. In that gesture, he taught us that there was nothing incongruous about bringing the Christ Child with us into the rest of the year.

It is a rich gift to a child to hear her father read the Christmas story, to see her father plan candlelight services so that people can worship on Christmas Eve, and to have her father compose a song, "Give Christ This Year." Now my father has crafted another gift -- a book of reflections and reminiscences about the high season of Christmas. Perhaps I will hear his words with greater love than any other reader. But in these pages you, too, can glimpse a little of this man and the birth of the Saviour he celebrates each December. May your life be enriched by these pages as mine has been by his life. ⭐

Lisa Carol Baker, PH.D., M.D.
Louisville, Kentucky

PREFACE

These brief reflections upon the Christmas season explain what I believe to be the very heart of the Christmas hope. Every line is meant to encourage, to inspire, to lift, to point toward the Bethlehem Star. Where matters of spiritual hope are concerned, I am an eternal optimist. How else can one interpret Christmas? Either God has broken into time to provide humanity a Saviour, or else we are a lost planet, destined to become a cinder heap. I choose to believe the former.

Christmas is important because it is important to God. He cares about all of us; of this I am sure! In every carol sung, every beautifully trimmed tree displayed, every gesture of goodwill expressed, and in every gift offered in His name, the message of Christmas is heralded forth.

Because of this incomparable love, we should keep not only the carols and unfading drama announced by heaven's entourage of angels, but also our own family traditions and customs as well.

Charles Dickens, in his book, *A Christmas Carol,* wrote "And it was always said of him, that he knew how to keep Christmas well; if any man alive possessed the knowledge. May that be truly said of us, and all of us." In so doing we present the magnificent heritage of a Christian Christmas to each new generation that they in turn might pass it on.

May I wish for you and those you love the most joyous Christmas ever... and remember

Give the gift of Christ this year.
Sing the song that brings you cheer,
Wrap it in a heart sincere
For all to know.
Every tree and steeple bell,
Leaves of holly-berries spell,
Snowflakes whisper and candles tell
Of God's great love.
Tell every boy, every girl you see,
Leave no one out, all God's gifts are free.
The manger gleams so invitingly
For you and me.
From any hillside you can find
Stars and Shepherds and things divine,
Happy angels blend in voice sublime,
*   Saviour's born.*

In Christian Love,

HOW FAR IS THE STAR?

wo thousand years and more have passed since Wise Men followed the guiding star to its tabernacling place in Bethlehem. What they experienced changed the direction of their lives forever. Since that grand discovery millions have found their way to the birthing place of Life Abundant. The virgin birth of Mary's baby, God's "only Begotten" has remained the unchanging median of hope in a world increasingly pagan.

Little wonder then that countless eyes look upward near Advent time, remindful of "no greater love," the gentle Saviour born. Pray, help us not to miss the Star in rounds of make believe, nor claim exclusiveness in someone's private Bethlehem. May we be forgiven our charade and games unworthy of believers blood-bound to lift up the Lamb of God. Deliver us, O Lord, from a Christmas man-managed, from tinseled trappings (however expensive!) magnifying the all too human trait to equate more for better, sound for sacredness, costumed splendor for the wonder of divine simplicity.

If indeed Christmas is for real, and we trust in God that it is, then the Star of Grace Abounding is never far away. You may see it in the trust of a child, the daring of dedicated youth. Perhaps you will see the star where colors blur in brothering, where deep commitment has led some kinsman with a caring heart to work unseen, unapplauded, in places unpronounceable; moreover, you may see the star beyond conventions staging in the place where a humble shepherd leads his sheep "beside still waters." This much I know...there will be no sight of the Christmas Star apart from the sight of the One whose incarnation we celebrate -- Jesus, the Invincible Lord!

The words of G. K. Chesterton seem particularly thoughtful in expressing the transcendency of the Christ of Christmas when he wrote, "There was a man who was born and dwelt in the East 2000 years ago and now I cannot look at a sheep or a shepherd, a lily or a cornfield, a raven or a sunset, a vineyard or a mountain without thinking of Him"... and may I most humbly add – a Star.

MY FAVORITE TIME OF YEAR

love Christmas. It's my favorite time of year. Every star and stable looks different because Christ came. Isn't it amazing what God did for mangers! And angels and miracles -- it's easier to believe in them at Christmastime. Don't ask me why. I'm not sure that I know. Perhaps at Christmas our thoughts turn more to others, or at least we get "caught up" in the spirit of giving and are blessed before we know it. Maybe it's the happy gathering of family and friends. Or it just might be, remember I said "might be," like the Shepherds of old, we have discovered The Child and have made a manger of our heart. That's it, isn't it? That's the superlative experience that makes this season different. God knew we needed Christmas. I love it. It's my favorite time of year.

TRYING TO KIDNAP CHRISTMAS

s I read about two youngsters who were dragging a large awkward sack through the toy department of a store, I could not keep from laughing. They were making a great deal of noise and were getting in the way of customers.

The manager approached. "Now boys," he admonished. "If you keep on being troublesome, Santa Claus won't come to your house."

"That's what you say," responded one youngster. "Who do you think we've got in this sack?"

One cannot help admiring the boys' determination, but Christmas is not something you can put in a sack. It cannot be kidnapped or held hostage from the world God made. Christmas is only meaningful when it is shared, when it is given away. Christmas is for everyone...everywhere...for all times. ⭐

MANGERS AND MIRACLES

arns and stables have seldom seemed inviting. I've never been much for mangers.. There is one exception, however -- the manger that held the Master. Somehow it has left an indelible mark on all of us, believers and unbelievers alike.

It seems strange that God's choice of a birthplace for His Son should be a lowly lean-to set apart from the crowded inn. Jesus could have been born in a palace, you know, with host illimitable ministering to His every need.

But the Father chose a stable-shelter built for lesser human things. In it, He gathered an unattended mother, a man stunned by wonder, and speechless shepherds kneeling in humble gaze.

I'm glad it happened that way, His coming, I mean. That's why Christmas has a uniqueness all its own. No other coming or coronation compares with it. The birth of Jesus marks history's watershed. Because He came, there is hope for every earthborn one of us.

For those who know and love the Christ Child, Christmas is more than evergreens in costumed loveliness, holly wreaths and sleigh bell sounds. It is more than packaged playthings, tables garlanded for feasting, the scent of bayberry, or even reflections at hearthside, however warm the glow.

Christmas is a gift from heaven for earth to enjoy. It is the announcement of a coming, the coming to earth of a Saviour, Jesus Christ. Christmas is the glorious Good News that mankind, all mankind of every race and nation, can experience forgiveness, freedom, and life abundant because of God's Gift, the Babe of Bethlehem.

I've never been much for mangers; but come to think of it, who is, until they know the "Miracle of Christmas"?

MAKING A CHRISTMAS LIST

ave you made your Christmas list this year? So often such a list is motivated more by obligation than opportunity to express Christian love. Often a gift list is an index to a person's character and concern. Why not plan your list as if you were giving in the very presence of the Christ of Christmas. Here are suggestions that will bring the warmth of a winter's fireside to your heart along with a much more Christ-like Christmas.

Give a gift to:

✔ your church

✔ the loneliest person you know

✔ the most generous person you know

✔ a person who has experienced a recent sorrow

✔ someone who would never expect to receive a gift from you

✔ someone who has been an encouragement to you this year

✔ someone you remember from the past who influenced or helped you at a special time

✔ someone who is likely to be overlooked at Christmastime

✔ a person of another color, religion or background

✔ someone who does not know about the Christ of Christmas

✔ someone to whom you remain completely anonymous.

While choosing your gift, remember that what people need most cannot be bought in stores. Do you suppose we give expensive gifts because we have forgotten how to express love?

Why not consider giving:

- ✔ a friendly phone call

- ✔ a letter of appreciation

- ✔ an hour of your time

- ✔ a happy disposition

- ✔ an interesting drive or nostalgic trip for a person who seldom can leave home

- ✔ a word of encouragement to some discouraged individual

- ✔ a visit to a hospital with small re-membrances for some of those who are ill

- ✔ your Christian faith, each day of the Christmas season

It is truly "better to give than to receive," and there is **never** a better time to give than **during the season of Christmas.** ☆

MERRY CHRISTMAS

erry Christmas! I love the sound of those words. They have always seemed to come more from heaven than earth. This greeting sounds of festive joy and brings goodwill by the heartful.

Merry Christmas! Don't dare miss the meaning of it all by being caught up in the packaging. Christmas is far more than a seasonal sales pitch or an inflated jolly old St. Nick. Christmas is not a time to place decorations around greed, tinsel around temptation, or imitation snow around an imitation faith. Christmas is for real. It's a carol of hope in a world of broken dreams, a guiding star for wanderers anonymous. It's the coming into time of the Saviour, Jesus Christ: a God-kind of joy lying in a manger; the Hope of Heaven in a mother's arms; man's second chance on a blanket of straw; and, thank God, Christmas did not end at Bethlehem.

This Child born of Mary grew up, lived as never a man lived, died upon a cross as never a man died, and He did it for every sin-blemished son of earth. More than that, He arose from a borrowed tomb more alive than ever before; and because of it, we know Christmas does not come from that which is under the tree, but from the One who died *on* the tree. It's not a gift; it's *the* gift. Christmas is something that happens to all those who believe deeply and everlastingly in the God who "so loved the world that He gave."

So, why shouldn't we be glad at Christmas and share the best news the world will ever hear? This is the kind of news that bankrupts bigotry, turns selfishness out as an unwelcomed tenant, and offers to brother all mankind.

Come now. Let us join hearts and voices, every believing one of us, and shout loudly enough for the whole world to hear. Merry Christmas! Merry Christmas to one and all!

THE JOY OF GETTING READY

here is a special excitement and anticipation in the days leading up to Christmas, the "getting ready" time. The children sometimes become "impossible." A great deal of investigative "house cleaning" is undertaken by certain members of the family with the ulterior motive of discovering that hidden gift or lay-a-way release. The time of "getting ready" is an important time. It puts the mental furniture in place and sets the stage for the commemoration of the greatest event this earth has ever known -- the coming of the Christ Child.

It is important that time be given to the preparation of heart and home. How tragic for an individual or a family to come to Christmas only to discover that they have missed it in the rush! I have seen some folk arrive for Christmas worship...nerves frayed, pocket-book empty, and spirits low, all because they had become so busy doing "things" they had left no time or energy for the most important matter of all -- adoring the Saviour.

Yes, there is a great deal to be said for "getting ready." It can make all the difference in your world!

IS IT A FAKE?

e was just a little boy of four. You would hardly think it would have mattered that much. But Jeff asked inquisitively, "Do you have your Christmas tree up yet?

"Yes," I replied.

"Is it a fake?" he asked.

"What do you mean?" I responded.

"I mean, is it a real tree or a fake?" Then I understood, and have pondered his childlike query times untold.

If reality is important to a four year old, how much more so should it be important to the rest of us!

We have grown accustomed to trickery, to masquerading in manners and morals. It is the "in" thing to see how much one can get by with. There is a certain intrigue in pursuing the pastime of trying to obtain something for nothing. Little wonder that "game" has rubbed off on the young and unaccountable.

His question was honest -- fair. It plumbed deeper than the Christmas tree and silenced the small talk of decorative trinkets. For in the innocent question of a child was heard the searching, haunting anxiousness of an unconvinced world. Is Christ for real? Do you truly believe that the Gospel is true? Is Christmas a stage play billed for a two-week run to be climaxed on December 25th? Is it a fake?

No doubt the uninhibited lifestyle of many professing Christians has led our worried world to wonder at the reality of the Miracle in a Manger. But when the whole of The Word is presented, when it is finally tested in the laboratory of human experience, there can be no doubt that Jesus Christ is for real. Whenever He has been allowed to enter, there is a difference. The blind see. The lame walk. The deaf hear. And yes, the dead in sin are being raised today as in all the yesterdays passed. He keeps on being born over and over again in the hearts of men and women. The Word becomes flesh again each time a soul is saved.

I, for one, would respond to the prophets of doom and the peddlers of doubt by insisting on the reality of the Christian hope. Christ is for real. Christmas is true. Jesus did come. He was born and placed in a manger, and He grew up. He lived as never a man lived and died as never a man died. But the greatest wonder of it all is that He arose from the grave to live forever as our great Eternal King. And now because He lives, Christmas is more than a day on the calendar. It is an experience in time that has made **every** day Christmas Day! Fake? No, not at all! If Christ be fakery, pray tell me what deserves the name reality!

CHRISTMAS: HOLLOW OR HOLY?

hristmas has always been a special time. I'm sure God intended it that way. After all, He planned the holy Child-birth long before the foundations of the earth were laid and long before the Spirit-seed grew in the virgin's womb.

Little wonder angels gathered to sing or that a chosen star drew close enough to light the way. Never before had earth known such a coming, and never again would a coming be so meaningful.

Christmas is God's gift to all of us; not just for the Wise Men and shepherds, the town folk of Bethlehem and the curious lodgers from the nearby inn, but for every one in all places, for all times...world without end.

It seems to me we need Christmas more each year. So many have grown hard, unbending, silent in sacred things. There's so little softness and gentleness these days. One fear stands out above all others; that we could come to Christmas with only a hollow faith inside a hollow heart. Tell me. What does one do with a hollow faith when confronted by life's imponderables -- broken dreams, pain and sorrow, the blight of human lostness?

I say man's thirsty soul calls out for Christmas. Nothing less than a firm faith in God will do. Heaven knows we've tried all the rest, and look at us: turning from one worldly carnival of flesh to another, sleeping past the sunrise of countless opportunities, gawking before the newest golden calf, reaching out to fondle the latest fad, and all the while knowing that God and God alone is the answer.

Then let Christmas come this year. Deliver us from the imitation, the superstitious, the costumed imagery of a produced Christmas. Instead, may we come to grips with the Miracle of Christmas morning, and may we do so with a full-orbed faith which believes that "God so loved the world, that He gave His only begotten Son, that whosoever believeth in Him should not perish, but have everlasting life." This alone deserves the right to be called Christmas.

HE CHOSE A STAR

hen God would show the way to Bethlehem He chose a star. Wise men followed the luminous beacon until they knelt before the baby Jesus. He could use a star today to show the way to the Saviour or a cloud or a rainbow. He could, should He deem it wise, mark the way by a cluster of cardinals in full flight or beam the manger-message via satellite. I say He could...but He has chosen another way.

You are that "other way." God has chosen to tell the "Good News" of the Saviour's birth through the company of the redeemed. His medium of delivery for sharing the greatest story ever told has been, is now, and will always be, the witness of believers who have found the message true. God has no other plan.

IT'S SO MUCH MORE!

n the haste of the Advent Season, don't miss what it's all about. Remember, it's Jesus' birthday, the time to honor Him and to adore the wondrous gift God sent to planet earth.

Christmas is more than a brightly trimmed tree, more than stacks of gifts waiting to be opened. Christmas is more than the aroma of freshly baked delicacies, or even Tiny Tim's "God bless us everyone." Christmas is something that God did in the world He made. It's the coming to earth of the Saviour who would save "His people from their sins." Christmas is hope in a mother's arms, a God-kind of joy lying in a manger. It is blind men seeing, demons put to flight, water turned to wine, withered hands restored, and the lame made whole. Christmas is forgiveness personified, loneliness befriended, and weakness fitted with wings. It's all of this and far more. Christmas is the red stain of Calvary and the borrowed tomb standing open...and empty. Christmas is God's answer for us all in the person of His Son, Jesus Christ. Is it any wonder the angels sang? How could they have contained the song?

HOLDING CHRISTMAS HOSTAGE

ave you noticed that there always seems to be a crisis at Christmas -- something frictional, separating, hurtful or demanding? It is as if the very forces of evil lay siege to the season that commemorates the birth of the Saviour. It was the same when Jesus came. Bethlehem was experiencing an acute housing shortage and offered little more than a cattle stall to serve as the delivery room for Mary's baby. Herod's mind ran murder-red with a plot to assassinate the little king. The infant Saviour was forced to become a refugee soon after his birth. Even the Wise Men from the East were pressed to find "another way" home, lest they encounter a despot's ambitious vengeance. Danger was no stranger to that first Christmas.

The similarity to our world of today is strikingly evident. Frightening tension and international confrontations test the mettle of every man's faith. World hunger promises death to multiplied thousands before year's end. Add to this the personal hurts, unbandaged wounds and broken hearts of millions more and you have the stage-set with Planet Earth brought into sharp focus.

How we need the message of Christmas this year! "There is born to you this day in the city of David a Saviour, which is Christ the Lord" is still the best news our world will ever hear. It remains the answer to personal peace and human understanding. Because it is the answer, we who know its wonder and worth dare not hold the Christmas message hostage in the world God made. We can, you know. Christmas can be held hostage by prejudice, pride, selfishness, exclusiveness, or by any number of other ways just as uncaring and unkind.

Let us stop standing guard over Jesus. He must be free of all man-made mangers to roam unhindered the roads of the Spirit's choosing. Surely after 1900 years we have learned that Christmas cannot be imprisoned in a place, restricted to a color, or held captive by any certain class or clientele. Christmas is God's good gift to all the world and cannot be kept under a tree any more than it can be hidden away in some nation's private Bethlehem. Thank God Christmas is for all of God's creations: heaven's answer to every man's crisis.

Christmas is for all of us...everywhere...for always.

CHRISTMAS BY CANDLELIGHT

andlelight is just made for Christmas, don't you think? I sometimes wonder why we are so intrigued by the candle's tiny light. Perhaps it is a luminous reminder of the words penned in the Bible's hymnbook, "For thou wilt light my candle, the Lord will enlighten my darkness" (Psalm 18:28). What a remarkable promise! No common taper of wax and string can hold contest to a candle's quiet flame. Little question that candles come into their own at Christmastime.

The radiant faith of unnumbered believers offers the candlelight of hope to those who walk the shadowed valleys, face the unexpected burdens of hurt and harm or stand in the chilling winds of temptation and doubt. It is the glow and glory of God's gift of Christmas that gives to life its essence, its meaningfulness. Oh, how we need the Christ of Christmas for days such as these!

Do not for a moment wonder as to the reach and depths of that common need. How dreadful indeed is the darkness of moral debasement, the utter tragedy of "man's inhumanity to man."

It is well within the bounds of truth to declare that this present darkness can never know a dawning apart from the person and finished works of Jesus Christ. He and He alone is the Light-Bringer, the reason for and purpose of the candlelight of Christmas.

We need it all -- the guiding star, shepherds keeping watch over their flocks, choiring angels. We need the sight of journeying Wise Men. Yes, and above all, we need the soul stirring reality of God's "Only Begotten," flesh-clad, lying in a manger.

I say we need Christmas just as it is -- the story of "grace so amazing," the coming to earth of the Saviour, gift-wrapped in simplicity and available to all. Surely we, the light-bearers of God's unrelenting love, should join heart and hands in the fervent prayer:

Holy Father, in the midst of this season of reverence, recollection and reverie, reveal the uselessness of wicks that bear no fire, the slow-burning and the satisfied. Remind us that candles are meant to be consumable, ex-pendable, never more than bearers of the borrowed glow.   Give us this year a Christmas that is kind, gentle, unselfish and sharing; one as lovely and precious as the trust of a child and, all the while, bold as Judah's lion.   May the Christ of Christmas turn us to meet the New Year with the Psalmist's song of confidence and joy,   "For thou wilt light my candle; the Lord, my God, will enlighten my darkness."

IN SEARCH OF CHRISTMAS

his is "the season to be jolly," so we are told. The annual barrage of media messages herald feature stories and footage calculated to stimulate bankable Christmas cheer, a reasonable amount of manufactured good will, and I must say a pretentious neighboring of sorts.

The usual invitational events of feasting and festivity mark the countdown of Christmas. Gridiron gods bring their gold, theater patrons their frankincense and the political opportunist their brown breath homage of myrrh. It's Christmas time, and untold thousands of the spiritually registered and unregistered (as the case may be) revert to childlike games:

> One gift for you;
>
> One gift for me;
>
> For after all,
>
> We bought the tree.

Little wonder so many search for the authentic Christmas. Genuine satisfaction stumbles over assembly-line saviours, cosmetic crosses and synthetic faith offered from a surrogate womb. Even we who know the mission of Mary's baby all too often fail to hear the choiring angels, save for their last refrain. More often still, we run a much slower pace than did the shepherds who came "with haste" to see the young Immanuel.

When will it finally dawn upon the ancestry of Adam that Christmas is not a destination but a celebration; it is not something outside to be searched for, but Someone nearer than breathing ready to be received and welcomed.

Christmas is not found at the end of the road to Bethlehem as if it were bonded to a place, held captive to color, kind or kin. Rather, Christmas is the collective joy that comes with the blessed seasonal reminder that we who truly trust in Jesus Christ as Saviour and Lord are by spiritual birth made family of the Child of Christmas morning.

That is what Christmas is about and that is where we shall find it -- resting strong and sure upon the foundation of inspired truth that declares, "The Word became flesh and dwelt among us." *Who, pray tell, would have it play the lesser part!*

AS SURE AS CHRISTMAS MORNING

e all need life's dependables, those unchanging landmarks and sheltering places where we can check our spiritual compass, review the bordering beyond which our hearts and heritage have chosen never to transgress.

Little about us is trustworthy, unbending, secure. Indeed, there are few dependables upon which we can lean come winds of winter. The maps of childhood's classroom have long since been remeasured. Quiet farmlands of yesterday are today's busy shopping centers. Ours is a nation on the move -- materially, mentally and morally. Children are called upon to adapt to new neighborhoods and family names as frequently as IBM introduces a computer change. Although the old sins have not changed, they have been updated and remain still as deadly barbed as before, but redressed with bright enticing new wire. The shared trust of common mission, one brother with another, no longer brings the

bonding once so undividedly treasured. Sad indeed but true, these are transitory times.

Where, pray tell, is there something, someone, some event, so indelibly calendared into time and eternity that one can count upon it, hope upon it, rest, if you please, upon its everlasting and absolute changelessness? Is there a source of absolute dependability?

The Christian faith reminds that such an answer is available. It is anchored in God, as creditable as His inspired word. Come closely, more closely still, until you can hear the gentle sound of heaven's holy encouragement:

"For unto you is born...a Saviour, which is Christ the Lord" (Luke 2:11). "For God, who commanded light to shine out of darkness, has shined in our hearts, to give the light of the knowledge of the glory of God in the face of Jesus Christ" (II Corinthians 4:6). "The peace of God, which passes all understanding, shall keep (stand guard over) your hearts and minds through Jesus Christ" (Philippians 4:7). "Hope we have as an anchor of the soul, both sure and steadfast...even

Jesus" (Hebrews 6:19-20). "Nevertheless, the foundation of God standeth sure, having this seal, the Lord knoweth them that are His..." (II Timothy 2:19).

Oh, yes, there is an answer! It comes from the *Book of Answers Everlasting*, to declare that Jesus Christ is the one unfailing source of certainty and supply. He is our blessed assurance...He is the Peace-Bringer.

We are now in the midst of the season that celebrates the Saviour's birth. Wonderful! Then let us do so with bells ringing and hearts singing. Let us do so with gifting, gathering and graciousness; but never must we forget that Christmas is more than a celebration, it is a certainty -- as sure as Christmas morning. This certainty allows every believer the right to say: "I know whom I have believed, and am persuaded that He is able to keep that which I have committed unto him against that day" (II Timothy 1:12).

Surely it is expedient and Christ-honoring at this Christmastime, that we join heart and hand with God's family, the whole world over, in saying: "Thanks be unto God for his unspeakable gift" (II Corinthians 9:15).

Marilyn Goss

HOME FOR CHRISTMAS

ome days ago I returned to the small Texas town of my birth. The landscape was the same; but being a confirmed sentimentalist, it came as somewhat of a shock that I had no home to come home to.

When "the old folks" began moving to their dwelling at 777 Heavenly Acres, there was no longer any need to keep the home place, or for that matter, all the reminders and relics that would in time become the gentle collectibles of children and grandchildren.

Changes had come with the years. The schoolhouse I attended as a child, always so indomitable and important, no longer existed. Its grounds had become the Little League field.

The thicket where I hunted "wild animals" and first joined the French Foreign Legion was now a trailer park.

Even the rusting Farm-all (International) Tractor, childhood's equation with power, no longer stood guard over the long unplowed back pasture.

Yes, the time had taken its toll upon the familiar marks of yesteryears. Imagine, no home to come home to.

Fortunately my faith found wings to rise above the momentary and to rest secured upon the magnificent thoughtfulness of God. Oh wondrous revelation!

Come closely and see what the "dayspring from on high" has left beneath the tree, Calvary's tree. He has left His children a home to come home to -- the church, precious place of love's abiding, commissioned instrument of grace so amazing.

Think of it. God has not only given to us the Christ of Christmas morning, but also He has given us a grace place, a gathering place, a welcoming place without restriction, be it color, class or circumstance.

God has given to us the church -- a home of blending, bonding and brothering for young and old alike. Its structure may change with the generations; its congregation may vary in likeness and location; its undershepherds may come and go; but the church remains constant, dependable, God's continuing gift -- a home to come home to.

How refreshing and encouraging it is to know that whenever the heart has an unquenchable longing for family and home, there is a home to come home to -- the church's throne gift of God's inexpressible and irrepressible love.

RECEIVE THE GIFT OF CHRISTMAS

ifts are not always easy to accept. I'm serious. The disposition to receiving graciously is very rare indeed. Never is this more truly illustrated than at Christmastime. The gift of a Saviour is so completely disarming. It devastates ego and shreds personal vanity.

Christmas, the "for real" Christmas, calls for the acceptance of all that God wants to give in exchange for all that our needs require. It is a celebration of "beauty for ashes," forgiveness for guilt, life for death, companionship for loneliness, access for alienation -- ten thousand joys for lack of assurance."

Confronted with the greatest example of divine grace the human heart can fathom, we are hard pressed to know how to react, how to accept "so great a salvation."

What does one do with the miracle of Christmas: ignore it, deny the reality of it, misrepresent it, abuse it, or accept it for what it is -- the Almighty's gift of the way to "Peace on earth" for every earth-born one of us?

I say let us accept the gospel of Christmas and inundate heaven with our praises. Let us receive it in worshipful adoration, join the likes of angels in singing, "Glory to God in the highest..." Relish the whole of it, every precious morsel of it. And why not? Christmas was meant to be celebrated.

Pray tell, how can the message of the incarnation be contained? Should we who know the Manger Child as Cross-Bearer, Grace-Conquerer, Hope-Bringer and Heart-Mender keep silent? It is certain the very stones would choir "Hosanna!"

It's Christmas. I love the very thought of it. Yes, and it's time, past time I fear, for all of us to join hearts and hands in celebration of the day "the Word became flesh and dwelt among us."

Come celebrate Jesus! "Ring the bells, ring the bells, let the whole world know. Christ was born in Bethlehem, many years ago..." Accept the gift of Christmas. God intended it so. ⭐

CHRISTMAS IS FOR REAL

et's not fault the unbeliever or the competitive marketplace for its offensive approach to Christmas. After all, holy things can only be understood in hearts where holy things have happened. Sooner or later everyone will realize that Christmas is for real; divinity is written all over it.

Christmas is not to be classified along with chances on a lake lot; an added amenity to the Super Bowl package. Never was it intended as the float of honor in Macy's Parade...not even Neiman Marcus' "ultimate gift."

Christmas is something God did in the world He made and through it He purposes to brother the likes of all mankind.

Indeed, Christmas is more than some slick, multicolored piece of junk mail, addressed to "Resident," certainly more than an impersonal number drawn for the "next in line." Christmas is the delivery room of hope authentic; the gathering place of praise unlimited.

Christmas is a personally addressed invitation engraved in scarlet with the most meaningful words, "There is born to you this day...a Saviour."

It is the perfect answer to the want ad column of millions who longingly search for someone just like Jesus. Christmas is God's good news for the first and the last person on earth.

Reality is difficult to deal with in a society conditioned by electronic laughter, manufactured snow and reindeer on demand. Sad to say, far too many prefer a synthetic scene -- the child stillborn, forever manger bound.

Deliver me from a Christmas ordered up like room service. No die-cast variety, please..

Instead, let Christmas come untainted, un-hewn. Free it from the cosmetics of pretension; the gray breath of faith half-grown.

I would come to Christmas confident that the mission to Bethlehem of Judea is a continuing mission...that Jesus Christ, God's only begotten, is still being born in the hearts of men and women wherever and whenever there are those who truly want a live-in Lord.

Should I be given a choice between a trade-marked nativity purporting "bigger than life" attraction or the simple one so lovingly described by Luke's fair pen, I would choose the latter. I'll have my Christmas real.

MAKE ROOM FOR MIRACLES

o one should fear a faith that makes room for miracles -- not if that faith has firmed itself on words inspired; not if that faith has come to brother where once there was no caring; not if that faith has plumbed the depths of human selfishness and returned to offer selfless giving in exchange.

It is such faith that sees the wondrous coming of the Saviour-child as God's miracle of Christmas. How else, pray tell, could such be understood or explained? If not the work of hands divine, then we worship before an artificial altar and hold to tinsel tied to a toy-like hope.

Forgive, dear Lord, should we who know the One who came to rest awhile on stable straw, be still in speaking of the incarnation. What greater news could come to cheer the heavy laden, the lonely, the lost? Oh, glorious truth -- the virgin's child, Immanuel!

Room for miracles? Indeed, there is room and more. I need them for such days as these. Enough of fleshly maneuvering, staged delusions, intravenous joy. Dear God, I have had my fill of that.

Let me go again to Bethlehem, to the fields where shepherds watched their flock, and let me feel the exhilarating expectancy of the angel's song. Yes, and if I can kneel vicariously with sheepmen near the newborn child, it will be but better still.

There is no greater gift than Christmas. "The Word made flesh" settled long ago the need to understand the treasury of grace. I praise His name and open wide my room for miracles. ☆

CHRISTMASTIME AGAIN

 am glad it's Christmastime again. We need it so this year. Somehow the forest where our churches grow appears more leafless than before, the trees of trust less frequent to come upon.

Remember how the spring ran swiftly by and summer's heat, like unkind words, waited days before it welcomed fall. Resultant scene: the praising ground lies fallow and unbroken, commissioned church is whispering, white fields remain unharvested.

I'm glad it's Christmastime again. We tend to believe more deeply this time of year. Faith comes without coaxing. Miracles are not the least uncommon.

The word we read is evergreen with promises sure as the Wise Men's star. Choiring angels and shepherds hastening to find the maiden holding hope in her arms seems not strange at all. Indeed, the stranger part is that such good news is harbored by the few.

I'm glad it's Christmastime again. We seem to love each other more at Christmastime. Not that it should be so. Nevertheless, there comes a bright and gentle caring, an allowing for imperfection, and a warm inviting kinship of togetherness that breaks out like a fever.

Have you noticed that it always comes when we find our way to the place of incarnation? Oh, the wonder that blessed Child has brought: peace-bringer, heart-mender, team-forger, promise-keeper, color-blender, brotherer and bridge-builder for all mankind.

What else, pray tell, could offer such reward, a greater joyfulness? The "Dayspring from on high has visited us," remaining still, sweet afterglow of God.

Time for Christmas? Yes, time and past. Ring all the bells. Fill the air with carols. Join hands that have not touched in years. Sound forth the reason to be merry. "There is born to you this day a Saviour, which is Christ the Lord." Glorious visitation, incarnate love, unspeakable gift, amazing grace -- it's Christmastime again. ☆

A CARING CHRISTMAS

hristmas can be a lonely time -- it can be if it is not shared, and if there are no people to fill spaces and give faces to the vacant hours. Such loneliness can come in crowds as well as in the empty place.

I am so very sure "care" was the motivation that brought God's Son to earth that first Christmastime; for in that one grand act of divine mercy, the Saviour offered companionship, hope, and peace to all who would receive Him.

There is far more to the nativity than inspiration for Christmas art and recollection of fond memories; much more than a favored chapter in a child's storybook. Christmas is the celebration of incarnation -- it is the Word, flesh-clad and breathing, feeling the hurts and harms of all mankind.

Christmas is a brothering, that lovely serendipity known to children of the King. Christmas is irresistible wonder, inexplicable grace, irrepressible joy. What God did in that

Bethlehem barn spelled L-O-V-E. Love, holy love, came calling to leave in its wake a manger full of gladness for every mother's child the whole world over.

Whatever else Christmas is, it is the announcement of God's caring love; and because of it, no one, (I repeat) no one, need ever be alone again.

We who are the benefactors of the manger miracle are not without responsibility.

Surely there are enough of us who believe deeply in the Child of Christmas Morning to offer Him - cradle, cross and all - to this desperately lost and lonely world. To care is to be like Jesus; and after all, isn't that what Christmas is about?

I WILL NOT LOSE HEART WITH CHRISTMAS

 will not lose heart with Christmas! Some will smile at the tiny shepherds kneeling beneath my tree and mock the store-bought likeness of a man-child in a maiden's arms. Indulge me as I wreath the scene in little lights of myriad colors, tie tinsel to the branches and fasten ornaments -- gentle reminders of all Christmases past. To know that once in a cattle stall it did happen so, does something warm and good inside me.

I will not lose heart with Christmas! The guns of harm are hardly silent, no less the unsolved demands of fevered minds. Decisions made at varied crossroads have left me breathless before each unwalked way. Yet through it all I've heard the clear, clear song of choiring angels singing: "There is born to you this day a Saviour..." And having heard, the harsh inequities that would have overwhelmed are strangely still.

I will not lose heart with Christmas! Giving has its place...and laughter. Please, no curfew on good cheer. Were silence under guard, the very stones themselves would shout their alleluias. Merriment is part and parcel of the news too wonderful to keep. Only, I could pray the gift God wrapped in stable straw might not be lost amid the packaging of coarse display. Dear Lord, forgive the haste that finds no time to wait before the wonder of it all.

I will not lose heart with Christmas! Fate has not dealt the blows, left wounds unhealed, dreams unrealized. No, something more than fate has handled the swift changing texture of the days just past. Such things but mark the length, breadth, height and depths of meaning kept inviolate beyond the human scene.

I believe God is, and that God knows best. Apart from this affirmation, life's riddle would leave me hesitant...alone...unsure. Thank God for Christmas -- Hope personified! Is it any wonder then that I am obsessed these days with every newborn child I hold. For once in a far away place, a baby came, the Word made flesh and nothing can ever be the same. ☆

ONCE UPON A CHRISTMAS

he King had come and Wise Men came bringing gifts -- gold, frankincense and myrrh. There's something about Christmas that insists on response. Choirs sing, bells ring, hearts cling to the good news that first was lent only to the lips of angels.

It was the news of divinity cribbed in a cattle stall, God's "only begotten" fleshed out and lying upon a blanket of straw. Breathtaking! Indeed, and how else could holiness be received? More awesome still, should human wonder be restrained?

The unresponsive are those who have outgrown miracles -- analyzers who have grown gray around the heartline, doubt-filled folk who no longer believe prodigals can come home, deviators who insist upon following the star of their choice which, not inconsequentially, may be nowhere near Bethlehem.

These are the ones who give no credence to the Incarnation. Of course not; that would be like believing rainbows follow the rain, that snowflakes are different by design or (something just as incredible) that red-winged cardinals are born to fly. Ridiculous! Is it really?

Of this I am certain. If Christmas were taken seriously, greed would lead a lonely life; selfishness would be on the endangered species list; abuse, violence, warfare and desperation would be left stranded at a point of no return.

It is fair to say Christmas brooks no kinship with dullness. It needs no credential or authenticity. Christmas is "joy come calling," God's grandest gift packaged in "love so amazing" and delivered to all humankind once upon a Christmas.

O, yes, I really do believe something holy happened that first Christmas. I believe every word of the story -- the song, shepherds, sheep, star and all. And I love what Christmas does within me and around me. For a brief time at least, kindness takes precedence over hostility and "Peace on earth" is deemed no uncommon dream.

Once upon a Christmas a child was born, and because of that birth, hope appeared with hands and feet; forgiveness smiled in Mary's arms; encouragement was dressed in swaddling clothes, and, for the very first time, the Life-giver had a face!

Once upon a Christmas the angels sang, "There is born to you this day, in the City of David, a Saviour, which is Christ the Lord " -- and nothing has ever been the same again!

CHRISTMAS: POSSIBILITIES UNLIMITED

hatever else Christmas brings, it brings a sense of overcoming -- the exciting promise of "possibilities unlimited." What a desperately needed gift! Here we are in the midst of manufactured bandaging, synthetic sympathy, impatient care, endless impossibilities. Apart from the Christmas announcement of God's divine intervening, we family of earthlings would be left without so much as a prayer.

That's why Christmas is so important: it offers the alternative to futility, the cloud-break through the storm. When God chose the maiden Mary to carry the Holy Child, He broke the barriers of life's impossibilities and put wings on all our dreams. Perhaps the whole of the Christmas wonder is gift wrapped in the words "For with God, nothing is impossible" (Luke 1:37). How deeply and how dearly those words penetrate the heart of every believer.

Nothing, absolutely nothing, shall be impossible because the "Word became flesh and dwelt among us" (John 1:14, RSV). No wound is unhealable, no loneliness unbearable, no mistakes irreparable, and no problem unsolvable. Ours is the God of unlimited possibilities, for "Neither death, nor life, nor angels, nor principalities, nor powers, nor things present, nor things to come, Nor height, nor depth, nor any other creature, shall be able to separate us from the love of God, which is in Christ Jesus our Lord" (Romans 8:38-39).

Why shouldn't we celebrate Christmastime? Pray tell me, how could our lips keep silent? I say thank God it's Christmas! The Cross-bearer and Peace-bringer has come; and because He has come, we will continue the journey whatever the turns of the road. Ours is no earthbound path, you know, for we are the children of God. And "with God, nothing shall be impossible."

WREATHS OF HOLLY --
WREATHS OF TEARS

e are in the midst of the Advent season. Common places are feeling the touch of uncommon thoughtfulness. While many are registering "the season to be jolly" with wreaths of holly, there are also those who display wreaths of tears.

I visited two homes this morning where death had come. Both families are faithful, Christ-loving families. One home displayed a beautiful Christmas wreath upon the door as a reminder of the coming of the Christ Child. I could not help but feel the strange and paradoxical congruency between the human need and the Nativity. In a spiritual sense they are inseparable. How could anyone face life's hurt and harm, the imponderables that leave one limp and soul weary, without the magnificent hope Christ's birth affords! Without the Incarnation, a walk through "the valley of the shadow" would be devastating indeed.

God knew how desperately we needed Christmas. Oh, how well He knew! I could walk away from those homes knowing full well that at any moment either wreath could be my own door's adornment. But because of the gift of the Saviour, I could also walk away with the calm assurance that the Christmas wreath offers salvation to the wreath of tears.

A CHRISTMAS CONFESSION

emember when we were children, how we yearned for that special gift at Christmastime? I suppose it can do no harm to confess that I searched every nook and cranny of my parental home for the sight of that box bearing my childhood dream gift. Now that the years have left me a lifetime of trinkets and treasures, and now that I have dutifully rendered the becoming expression, "It's just what I've always wanted!", I think it's time to let it be known what I really, really, want for Christmas this year.

Most of all I want Christmas to ring with a clear, fresh note of hopefulness, a believable, credible, "take it to the bank" kind of hope. Forget the animated froth of current vintage. No generic Jesus, please! Deliver me from the deluge of look-a-like shepherds, and even the borrowed baby straight from the Christmas crib. Should this sound of sacrilege, forgive. Come nearer and hear more clearly.

I would not take away a single thread from the swaddling cloth that wrapped the tiny infant fresh come from God, or knowingly find fault with any pure adoration expressed through decoration. How dearly I have loved and do love the captivation, color, and concentric circles filled with blessed reminders of the Incarnation; nevertheless, one can relish all the happy sounds and songs of Christendom, all the religious revelry, and all the breathtaking beauty of manufactured merriment and still miss the reason the Baby came.

Try hard to understand. I contend that we are famishing in the rush that leaves little time to stand in awe of the simplistic wonder of Christmas. The pageantry of inspired revelation, the birth of hope, is far too often the expendable of Christmas.

The season of Christmas is the best time ever to bring our families to the gathering place, the Father's house. Bring them not for what they can see, but for what they cannot see, the reality of the invisible. Bring them not for what they can hear, but that they may listen for "the still, small voice of God." Bring them to the Father's house not to touch the nativity, but to be touched by it, to learn the continuing truth that the Child of Mary grew up, died upon a cross of wood, was buried and arose from a tomb that could not hold Him! Herein lies Christmas at its best!

For such hope I plead my guilt and offer this sincere confession. Little wonder I love Christmas, for "tis the season" my hope wears wings.

THE CHRISTMAS OF '76

shall never forget it -- the Christmas of '76. By all human calculations it appeared to have the prospects of being a most depressive, lonesome, and difficult time. Not that there was any serious illness or family problem lurking in the corners of this December. It was just that we had always been together at Christmas -- all the family, that is. Now, for the first time, our children were scattered, literally scattered throughout the world. Dick, our eldest son, was in Greece working with a film company. David was in Switzerland at L'Abri studying with Dr. Francis Schaeffer at his student retreat, and Lisa was in Perdue University continuing her graduate work. Both boys would be unable to be home. We had contented ourselves as best we could with the thought that at least we would have Lisa for this special season.

Tradition saw the Baker clan gathering at the homeplace in Farmersville. My brother and his wife and children had already arrived when we drove up the drive to be warmly welcomed by my mother and father. It was obvious that we were all less than enthusiastic about the prospects of the family dinner and the Christmas tree gifting that would be entered into without our two boys.

There was the usual banter, food tasting, and table setting. I suppose we were pretending to be a bit more "merry" than usual. When it appeared that everything was in readiness for us to start on the multiple treats that were spread on grandmother's table, I heard someone say, "Wasn't that the doorbell?" It was then that I turned to see Dick, our eldest son who supposedly was in Greece, come smiling through the front doorway. Only another parent can imagine the change that started coming over that household.

There was the rush to the front door, everyone talking at once, embraces and kisses; all underscored by the statement, "Where in the world did you come from? You are supposed to be in Greece. Why didn't you tell us you were coming?" This might have gone on for several minutes had there not been a knock at the back door. *And*, this you will never believe. As my brother opened the back door in answer to the knock, who should be standing there grinning like the proverbial possum but David (who, I might add, was supposed to be in Switzerland!). If you thought the first son's entrance started bells ringing in the Baker household, can you imagine what happened when the second son arrived, totally unexpected...and as you know, so perfectly "arranged" to their advantage!

It is unnecessary to continue this story. For those of you who share and understand parental love, no further explanation is necessary. The Christmas of '76 will always remain unforgettable in our memory. That was the year our "prodigals" came home from their wandering. That was the year we had to arrange quick gifts for the tree. That was the year we came to understand again that Christmas is more than a toy or a roasted turkey or time away from one's normal routine. Christmas is being together...together with those you love. Oh, yes, I'll never forget the Christmas of '76.

SINCE CHRISTMAS CAME CALLING

It's never been the same...not since Christmas came calling. How could it be? Never before had humanity been left such a heart full of hope, such reason for inspiration, such an awesome experience: a God with a face. And, as if that were not enough, never before had mankind been offered promises surer than the guiding star to claim in needful hours. All this and more since Christmas came to call.

Is it any wonder that the angels sang and shepherds came? Hardly. For with the advent of God's "Only Begotten" came grace personified, goodness resting on a blanket of straw and celestial glory wrapped in swaddling clothes.

Since Christmas came calling, prodigals and wanderers can come home and find welcome -- the bruised and broken, a place of repair.

Since Christmas came calling, believers' graves are garlanded in fresh evergreen and gone forever is death's frightful sting.

So meaningful the phrase "since Christmas came calling." Forgive, dear Lord, should we mortals miss the majesty of Christmas or fail to grasp the breathtaking splendor of it all!

Read again the old, old story in Luke 2:8-11. We need to hear it so desperately today. Heaven knows we've drifted far enough and sunk low enough!

Let us read the gospel story again and again until that sweet Child who once lay warm in Mary's arms lies resting warm and comfortably in our hearts. Dare we forget that in Christ and Christ alone, is found the full message of joy God has so bountifully provided "since Christmas came calling."

CHRISTMAS IS FOREVER

or many, the countdown for gifting has begun. In a few short hours families will gather for merriment and feasting; the air will be full of the joyful sound of excited children, the sights and happiness that follow the distributing of gifts. By late evening, December 25th, the Christmas tree will already be looking lonely, its packages stripped away like autumn leaves. Yes, and far too soon for some, there will be embracements of farewell, return journeys homeward, and a storehouse full of new memories for all the years to come. Christmas will have come and gone.

Come and gone, that is, if it is little more than the exchange of gifts or a family holiday, or left-over bills to pay. Come and gone, that is, if it leaves us with nothing more than a naked tree and a naked heart. But if this Christmas is Christian, and I pray to God that it is, then it is still Christmas on December 27 and 28 and all the other days and years that are ahead. For God's manger-born Son did not remain to be a prisoner of sentiment; He would not condescend to be merely the cosmetic Christ on Caesar's tax role. Rather, God's Only Begotten grew up. He not only showed the way to heaven, He made the way; making a Christmas out of Calvary and a testimony of triumph out of Joseph's new tomb.

Christmas can never be over for the believer. Since that holy thing happened in the cattle stall at Bethlehem, it can never be night again. And because it happened, Christmas is forever.

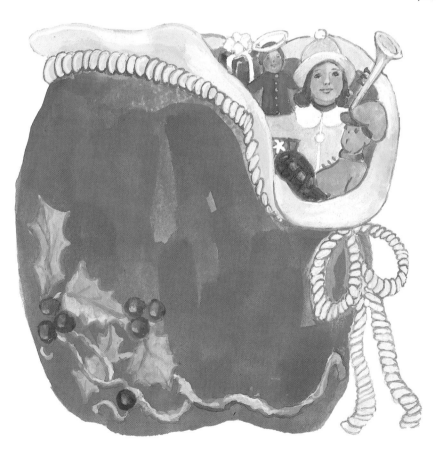

THERE'LL ALWAYS BE A CHRISTMAS

So long as truth remains in trust,

Conceived with promise held inviolate;

So long as faith confirms the birth

Of Day Spring's glad arriving;

So long as Wise Men find the star,

And Shepherds know where angels are;

So long as gifts are brought with care,

And joyful laughter fills the air;

So long as hope responds in kind,

To share till breathless news divine;

So long as children dream their dreams,

Of lions and lambs in single ring;

So long as streets are free from hate,

Where young and old can congregate;

So long as fields awake to green,

Long Winter's wind still welcomes Spring,

So long as angels anthem sing,

And Virgin's child is crowned the King --

There 'll always be a Christmas.

BO Baker
3-12-96

THE CHRISTMAS STORY

A Saviour Promised

And in the sixth month the angel Gabriel was sent from God unto a city of Galilee, named Nazareth, to a virgin espoused to a man whose name was Joseph, of the house of David; and the virgin's name was Mary.

And the angel came in unto her, and said, Hail, thou that art highly favoured, the Lord is with thee: blessed art thou among women.

And when she saw him, she was troubled at his saying, and cast in her mind what manner of salutation this should be.

And the angel said unto her, Fear not, Mary: for thou hast found favour with God. And, behold, thou shalt conceive in thy womb, and bring forth a son, and shalt call his name JESUS.

He shall be great, and shall be called the Son of the Highest: and the Lord God shall give unto him the throne of his father David:

And he shall reign over the house of Jacob for ever; and of his kingdom there shall be no end.

Then said Mary unto the angel, How shall this be, seeing I know not a man?

And the angel answered and said unto her, The Holy Ghost shall come upon thee, and the power of the Highest shall overshadow thee: therefore also that holy thing which shall be born of thee shall be called the Son of God.

Luke 1:26-35

The Visit of the Wise Men
Now when Jesus was born in Bethlehem of Judea in the days of Herod the king, behold, there came wise men from the east to Jerusalem,

Saying, Where is he that is born the King of the Jews? For we have seen his star in the east, and are come to worship him.

When Herod the king had heard these things, he was troubled, and all Jerusalem with him.

And when he had gathered all the chief priests and scribes of the people together, he demanded of them where Christ should be born

And they said unto him, In Bethlehem of Judea: for thus it is written by the prophet,

And thou Bethlehem, in the land of Juda, art not the least among the princes of Juda: for out of thee shall come a Governor, that shall rule my people Israel.

Then Herod, when he had privily called the wise men, inquired of them diligently what time the star appeared.

And he sent them to Bethlehem, and said, Go and search diligently for the young child; and when ye have found him, bring me word again, that I may come and worship him also.

When they had heard the king, they departed; and, lo, the star, which they saw in the east, went before them, till it came and stood over where the young child was.

When they saw the star, they rejoiced with exceeding great joy.

And when they were come into the house, they saw the young child with Mary his mother, and fell down, and worshiped him: and when they had opened their treasures, they presented unto him gifts; gold, and frankincense, and myrrh.

And being warned of God in a dream that they should not return to Herod, they departed into their own country another way.

Matthew 2:1-12

The Birth of the King

And it came to pass in those days, that there went out a decree from Caesar Augustus, that all the world should be taxed.

(And this taxing was first made when Cyrenius was governor of Syria.)

And all went to be taxed, every one into his own city.

And Joseph also went up from Galilee, out of the city of Nazareth, into Judea, unto the city of David, which is called Bethlehem; (because he was of the house and lineage of David:)

To be taxed with Mary his espoused wife, being great with child.

And so it was, that, while they were there, the days were accomplished that she should be delivered.

And she brought forth her first-born son, and wrapped him in swaddling clothes, and laid him in a manger; because there was no room for them in the inn.

Luke 2:1-7

The Song The Shepherds Heard

And there were in the same country shepherds abiding in the field, keeping watch over their flock by night.

And, lo, the angel of the Lord came upon them, and the glory of the Lord shone round about them: and they were sore afraid.

And the angel said unto them, Fear not: for, behold, I bring you good tidings of great joy, which shall be to all people.

For unto you is born this day in the city of David a Saviour, which is Christ the Lord.

And this shall be a sign unto you; Ye shall find the babe wrapped in swaddling clothes, lying in a manger.

And suddenly there was with the angel a multitude of the heavenly host praising God, and saying,

Glory to God in the highest, and on earth peace, good will toward men.

And it came to pass, as the angels were gone away from them into heaven, the shepherds said one to another, Let us now go even unto Bethlehem, and see this thing which is come to pass, which the Lord hath made known unto us.

Luke 2:8-15

ABOUT THE AUTHOR

BO Baker is a much sought after Churchman, international evangelist, author, lyricist, and denominational statesman. He was named a Distinguished Alumni by Southwestern Baptist Theological Seminary, recipient of Baylor University's James Huckins-Baylor Founders Day Award, and its prestigious W. R. White Meritorious Service Award. In recognition of his leadership and world wide ministry, the Doctor of Divinity degree has been conferred upon him by Dallas Baptist University (1971) and Baylor University (1988).